Make Us See

Make Us See

Prayers and Meditations

N.C. Clair

Edgehill Publishing
Ann Arbor, Michigan

Make Us See: Prayers and Meditations

Copyright © 2015 by N.C. Clair.

Cover and interior design by Stephen Caine
Photo by N.C. Clair

ISBN: 978-0-692-57698-4

Published by Edgehill Publishing
Ann Arbor, Michigan
(818) 744-0806

Printed in the United States of America

10 9 8 7 6 5 4 3 2 1

Contents

Prayers

Meditations

Preface

This book is offered as a resource for the spiritual life. It is my firm conviction that the Christian faith, rightly understood, is one that grounds the "spiritual" squarely in lived experience. In other words, Christian faith is an "earthed spirituality".

This grounding in lived experience has many implications, but there are two primary issues at stake for me that pulse through the content of these prayers and meditations. First, the Christian faith is an ongoing conversation about how to live fully in the here and now because it's central claim is that God in Christ has irrevocably affirmed the here and now of material existence by taking on materiality as the human, Jesus of Nazareth. Furthermore, the Christian vision of the last things, the eschaton, is one that robustly affirms a final state where this material realm becomes the eternal dwelling place of God. This is indisputable. Second, the Christian faith inculcates "a way of seeing" because of God's generous affirmation of the material world via the Incarnation. Our spiritual lives are more than an exercise in superior ethics, or the pursuit of virtues, and the attainment of the good life. It is faith as a vision of God that is chosen by us to be the framework upon which we construct the lives God has given to us as gift.

The Christian way of seeing (which is just another way of saying "faith") affirms materiality, the robust flourishing of life, and is supremely confident of God's pervasive presence in all things, at all times. Whether consciously held by us or not, this vision is consistent with the ancient Christian understanding of God's presence mediated via the Creation, in the fabric of lived experience. It takes seriously the claim found in Scripture that we live and move and have our being in God. As a result, the basic stance of those who see rightly is one of seeking, listening, humble openness to the possibility of God in every circumstance, and a readiness to receive that Presence wherever it is found.

It is my hope that the writing found in this volume reflects a pastoral desire for people of faith to see God, and our lives, rightly. Furthermore, it is also my hope that this resource will give the reader language to express that vision in their own spiritual life.

These prayers have been collected over more than a decade of ministry in a variety of Christian faith communities. They were initially created for a variety of purposes. Some come from personal reflection, others were designed for the preaching moment, and still others were written for corporate expressions of worship. All are devotional.

No book is a solo effort in its inspiration or production.

My deepest gratitude belongs to my wife, Jill Clair. She tirelessly encouraged me to have the confidence to share my writing, and she possessed the expertise that guided the production of this volume. An author herself, she is an amazing entrepreneur, a fantastic mom to our three girls, and the best life partner I could ever imagine. To say that I love her would be an understatement of vast proportion.

A great thanks also belongs to my parents, Craig and Dorothy Clair. Both of them modeled to me a deep confidence in the reality and availability of God. My father's deep sense of God's grace and love for each human being, his moral clarity and perception, and basic posture of awe for the Christ whose love redeems, these are real gifts to me. My mother's kindness, compassion, constancy, faithfulness and simple, uncomplicated devotion to Jesus are the quiet ballast of her character and continue to call me to a better way.

It would be a great oversight if I failed to acknowledge the influence of Dr. John Thatamanil. While at Vanderbilt Divinity, he gently challenged me to value the positive resources of my evangelical heritage even while encouraging the growth of my theological vision and voice. His own example of robust spiritual practices and awareness, humor, rigorous thinking, moral imagination, and creativity continue to inspire me even as I aspire to follow his example as a growing theologian.

Other key voices during my Nashville sojourn were John Mogabgab and Pamela Hawkins. As the editorial leadership of Weavings Journal, they not only welcomed me as their intern, but also affirmed my call and gifts for ministry. Their faithful presence, clarity of purpose, sense of place, humility and friendship were a means of grace in my life.

The people of Huron Hills Church in Ann Arbor deserve my gratitude for their acceptance, love and encouragement. It is a privilege to serve within a community that frees me to be who I am in my vocation, challenges me to grow, and allows me to do the same. I've found a place to preach, lead and worship that is filled with a relentless commitment to the life and mission of King Jesus.

N.C. Clair

South Downs Abbey
November 2015

Prayers

O Light

O Light,
Fulsome and penetrating,
yet imperceptible in altar candles
and colored sanctuary glass.

Shine. Shine in hearts and minds;
warming our earthen frames,
making us alive to life and to live.

O Light that makes darkness leave,
disperse the veiling shadows to which we cling;
graciously disturb us and make us see.

Make us see that we are not our darkness,
our shadows, our regret or pain.

O Light of dancing Three,
we sing your God-head,
your gleaming realness born to us.

Your healing issue to the human race,
illuminated in us, is now ours.

Amen.

At Daybreak

Lord,
Let my mind be peaceful,
let my words be kind,
let my heart be loving.
Amen.

—*Thom Dawkins*

You are Life

My God,
You are Life and fully present to me.

I find You in all things and every moment.
In stars and sunsets, in breezes and thunder,
in laughter and celebration, in work and silence,
You are with me.

You are my only good, my only treasure.
Wild and free, You are the generous and extravagant Lover.
For You I am desperate. With You I am consumed.

Alleluia. Alleluia. Alleluia.
Amen.

More & Less

O God,
give us more. And less.
More of what we need,
less of what we want.
More on our knees,
less on our soapboxes.
More of our ears,
less of our lips.
More loving,
less fear.
More doing right,
less "being right".

Amen.

Lament

God,
We are uncertain, unsure, and unclear.
When will You speak to us?
When will Your voice be heard?
Remember us, gentle us, hold us close.

Darkness is sweeping over us
and even the joys of life are muted and fading.
When will we hear Your songs of joy again?
We crave Your presence.

We are empty and dry.
We have no words. We are broken.
How can we explain our losses and our wounds?
But You see and understand.

We have our hope in You, Silent God.
We have known You in Your speaking.
So come and speak again, creating again,
and we will be saved.

Our God is the God who heals.
Our God is the God who speaks.
Our God is the God who makes alive.
Our God is the God of vindication.

Let all people praise You.
Even with tears we will praise You.

Amen.

Divine Presence

Divine Presence,
lead me away from the "simple battles" of life—
bills, schedules, housework.

Take me to the deepest deserts and wrestle me to the
ground. Make of me what You have seen in long eternity
past. And let me see that even in Your hidden purposes, I
still can know that You are there.

Amen.

Help Me

Holy One,
Help me to be honest with You when I need to be.
And teach me to trust that Your unruly, untamed Spirit
is for my good.

Amen.

Speaking God

Speaking God, un-stop our ears.
Moving God, un-blind our eyes.
Healing God, un-harden our hearts.

For You have the words of life.
You have the power to heal and transform.
You have promised us new hearts.

We are ready to listen.
We are ready to see.
We are ready to change.

Amen.

Almighty Father

Almighty Father,

Dwell with us, Your people.

Cause us to draw near to You even in the midst of our failures. In Your presence help us to find a God who is waiting with open hands and heart to receive us as we return to you.

Amen.

after I Kings 8:14-61

God Who Does Not Forget

God Who Does Not Forget,
Remember us, even as we fail to be mindful of You.
Help us to celebrate the shutting door as a means of Grace
from Your Hand—Your Presence deeply involved in the
details of our lives.

Amen.

after Genesis 7:11-8:5

God of Glory

God of Glory,
Deliver me from doubt.
Enlarge my heart to store up a trove of remembrances
of Your promises and provision.

Teach me to be mindful of Your presence
even when I am stuck between an army and an ocean.

Amen.

after Exodus 14

Confronter and Questioner

Confronter and Questioner,
Hold before us the mirror of Your stark questions.
Give us the courage to face what we behold.
And in the wake of what we see, we are assured the
gift of humility, birthing in us a desire to ask and listen
more than one to declare and speak.

Amen.

Reconciler

Reconciler,
Heal me.
Heal us. And enlarge our hearts to receive Your
tenderness and grace.

For the sake of Your wounded Son,
Amen.

Directing God

Directing God,
Send us into a way
of provision and stewardship for all people—
even those who wrong us.
Free us into a bondage that
enlarges Your purposes in our lives.

Amen.

Binding God

Binding God,
Bind our hearts together with all people.
Cleave us to You and surprise us as we discover all
people in that place of restless hearts made peaceful.

Amen.

Praise Be To You

Praise be to You, Creator of all things.
Giver of Life.
Sustainer of all things.
Ever creating, ever loving.

Praise be to You, Lord Christ, Wisdom of the Godhead.
God incarnate, revealed.
God spoken, heard.
Apprehended, yet incomprehensible.

Praise be to You, Holy Breath.
God's presence that illumines our darkened minds.
The passion of the Godhead that fires our hearts.
The very power of Divinity en-gracing us to live.

Praise be to You, Mysterious Three who are One in Love.

In Your eternal life we live.
In Your holy dance we move.
In Your being we have our being.

Amen.

Renunciation

God,
Show me all the ways that I seek power for myself.
I will renounce them.
Teach me Your ways.

Amen.

Abandoned One

Abandoned One,
Call us to abandon our refusal to accept from Your hand the good and the difficult. Give us the strength to acknowledge You as God in every moment.

Amen.

after Isaiah 54:7

Dream Giving God

Dream Giving God,
Teach us to trust while in the well of despair.
Teach us to trust while betrayal surges.
Teach us to trust while traveling to our Egypt.
Keep us in dreams even if we are kept in slavery.
Teach us to trust and dream again.

Amen.

after Genesis 37

Exalted One

Exalted One,
Deepen within us a sense of expectation for Your elevating spirit. Abide with us in all things, and in all places, that we might serve You with gratitude and joyfulness of spirit.

Amen.

after I Samuel 16:1-13

Burning Presence

Burning Presence,
Be present with us in our exiles and our deserts.
Speak forth a calling and a promise.
And clothe our beings with courage to trust again.

Amen.

after Exodus 13 and Malachi 3:1-4

Jesus Full of Trust

Jesus,
Full of trust in Your Father, teach me to trust like You.
Give me courage to gaze upon Your face
without swerving to the left or right;
or, worse yet, to turn around
and head away from Your presence.

In You we see the Father who mothers us.
Help me leave off any image of God
that does not align with Your example,
no matter how pious or right they appear.

Jesus,
Full of trust in us, Your friends.
Teach me to trust others like You do.
Give me courage to believe what You see in us is real.
In You, we see each other—a seeing beyond sight.
It is a way of knowing You revealed in every person.

Amen.

God Who Is

God Who Is,
Inspire in us a passion to know You more.
Give us words to bless our enemies.
Heal our hearts with courage to see and ask
for what You have said is ours.

Amen.

God Who Speaks

God Who Speaks,

Help me not to miss Your words even when they are in the mouth of my enemy. Teach me to trust that You are ever present--speaking, directing and guiding.

Bless us all with courage to truly hear and move.

Amen.

Tester & Provider

Tester and Provider,
Test me and gently reveal my need for Your provision.

Ground me in You—the One who is—that I might know
what I am, by Your grace, for Your glory, and Your greater
purposes.

Amen.

Restorer

Now You, Restorer,
Now You restore us to life again.

Rejoin our scattered bones and our shattered bodies.
Re-incarnate, re-build, re-make us.

Put Your Spirit in us and we will live.
Settle us and we will know You as You are.
And these dry bones will dance.

after Ezekiel 37:1-14

You Called

You called.
So I am coming, I am becoming. I am believing.
I am breathing. I am seeing.
I am listening. I am hearing. I am thirsty. I am drinking.
I am Living. I am singing.
I am moving. I am dancing. You are with me.
I am laughing.

First Lazarus, now me.
Amen.

after John 11:33-44

Vision

Vision,
Enlarge our sight to include the dimensions of the
depth of Your presence in our everyday, in our good,
our horrific, our sublime, our ridiculous.
And enliven our minds to comprehend what it is we see,
that we may be marked by You and bear the marks of
Your life in our own.

Amen.

Shock Us With Grace

Surpriser and Surprise,
Shock us with grace.
Astonish us with love.
Overwhelm us with mercy.

Amen.

after Isaiah 58:8a

Shepherd's Prayer

"The Lord is my shepherd, I lack nothing".

Shepherd-God, tend me
You bring me to rest because I can't rest on my own—
I won't rest on my own.

And over waters like glass and diamond You nourish
my "me", the me You dreamed me to be, Your "me".

Your direction is correct for Your reasons and for Your
purposes. So even "my journey" is really not about me, but
You. You are telling a story about Yourself—the God of Love.

If the steps I take then lead to places of:
chaos,
confusion,
even death,
there will be no real cause to despair.

You have led me and You will lead me.
Regardless of the challenge I know You're going first
into the fray.

You are more than able to protect, repair and rescue
me when things get rough.

You celebrate, provide, and bless me before all who would
destroy me. You vindicate me as Your own before my
enemies, because You've made them Your enemies too.

I am created to an empowered purpose and You have
lavished a continual source of strength and never-ending
refreshment on me.

Nothing but blessings in my wake!
Nothing but health and joy shall come of my endeavors!

With You is my rest.
In Your place, as You live, so shall I live with You.
Amen.

after Psalm 23

Sending

Heavenly Father,
Send me forth bearing Your life into the world again.
Every day, may I be the place of Your nativity
in deeds of compassion and words of kindness,
with a heart of patience and a tender spirit.

Amen.

Doxology

Praise God from whom all blessings flow.
Praise God for friends who sing praise
in times of trouble.
Praise God for the hearts of those that love me.
Praise God for passionate worship.
Praise God for change and new beginnings.
Praise God for strength of conviction and vision.
Praise God for honesty.
Praise God for the revelation of heart desire.
Praise God for new found joy.
Praise God. Praise God. Praise God.
Praise Him all creatures here below.
Praise Him above you heavenly host.
Praise Father, Son and Holy Ghost.

Amen.

Meditations

The Beckoning Absence

A few years ago I was invited by a parishioner to speak with a friend of hers who did not attend our congregation. Her friend's husband had been in a coma for seven years after emergency heart surgery. He was being sustained only by a feeding tube and his doctors were talking with his wife about the possible withdrawal of the tube because there had been no sign of improvement for such a long time. Understandably, she was experiencing distress and confusion.

When I met with her, I asked if she had also sought counsel from her own pastor. She responded that she wasn't seeking pastoral advice from me, just a listening ear from someone who would not push her toward a decision. It became apparent as I listened to her story that while the doctors were talking about ending her husband's treatment, her pastor and other church members were questioning the strength of her faith and Christian commitment if she even considered letting the doctors do so.

As I sat with her, she tearfully related the tragic account of her husband's illness, followed by the story of their relationship, their life together, children and grandchildren, favorite trips, and moments when they leaned on each other "to get through." She ended our conversation by asking if I would visit her husband in the hospital. I agreed, and she then thanked me as we parted ways.

The next day I went to the hospital accompanied by two ministry interns from my congregation. Although I justified their presence as a learning opportunity for them, I knew that I really wanted moral support for what I anticipated would be a difficult visit. When we entered the coma wing, we saw her husband almost immediately. His bed was close to a door away from the floor-to-ceiling windows, but still bathed in natural light. He was a large man, curled up on his side like a child in peaceful sleep. As the interns waited near the foot of his bed, I went to stand at his side, took his hand in mine, and greeted him by name. The easy, natural rise and fall of his breathing was his only response.

Waiting in the quiet with him, my eyes began to take in his surroundings. What most captured my attention was a bulletin board hanging on the wall above his bed. There, in great personal detail, was posted seven-years' evidence of the tragic loss and deep love felt by this man's family. From corner to corner, the board was packed with seven years' worth of cards and photographs. There were school pictures of his grandchildren, favorite photos from the trips I'd heard about, and on every available inch of space there were cards. Card after card after card. Birthday cards. Anniversary cards. Valentine's Day cards. Get Well cards. Just Thinking of You cards. Some were from his children, some from his grandchildren, but most were from his wife with a special note from her inside each one. "I am who I am because of you. I love you," she had written in a card tacked wide open for all to read. As I leaned over for a closer look, I suddenly realized: it was that year's anniversary card celebrating almost thirty years together. And in those few words written to the man she loved I sensed a quiet, insistent faith—a faith that would not countenance the idea that the last seven years of coma had stolen anything from her, from them.

Then, after I finished reading the note and moved away from the bulletin board, one of the interns, with pain and confusion in his voice, asked, "Where is Jesus in this? Where is God in a seven-year coma?

I believe it is one of the spiritual life's few certainties that, at some time, we will experience the absence of God. We may sense this absence as a personal experience of abandonment, or, like that intern, as a question that arises when we observe the suffering of another. When God seems absent to us, we may come to see only shadow and hear only silence. In the presence of the inescapable and often painful ambiguity of human existence, there has always been a stream of theological reflection in Christian tradition that wrestles with the absence of God.

This wrestling can be critical to our life of faith. The experience of God's absence may drive us to look directly at the ineffable, unruly, untamed character of the Source of all things. God's absence moves us beyond ourselves and our failing conceptions of God, raising the possibility that they may be only idolatrous fabrications. In the course of wrestling with the absence of God, the viability of our limited images and faltering defenses of God come to an end.

The Absence is the silent, resounding "No" in which God refuses to give an accounting of God's Self on our terms and act according to our wishes. In the jarring seasons of God's absence we encounter a blinding darkness that invites and strangely enables us to see God beyond our images of the Divine. In this way, the experience of God's absence is an answer to Meister Eckhart's famous prayer: "I pray God to rid me of God."

The invitation to look upon God in this way is therefore an invitation to faith. It is in our faithful and faith-filled insistence that God is present, even when we cannot see or hear God, that God is mysteriously made known as present. This faithful and faith-filled resistance to absence is, paradoxically, a witness to the God in whom we live and move and have our being—the God who empowers our resistance when it makes no apparent sense to resist in the first place.

We are neither alone in this insistence nor futilely resisting the fragmenting impact of God's absence. No, there is One who, in the Incarnation, makes plain in spite of all our anguished ruminations that God will never leave or forsake us. In the person of Christ we meet the Great High Priest who knows our struggles, our pain, our experience of emptiness and abandonment. In Christ, God's knowledge of us is immeasurably more than an example of divine encyclopedic omniscience. Rather, in Christ, God's knowledge as Creator transcends itself as God takes our own lives into the intimacy of God's own life.

Jesus Christ, incarnate God and fully human, stands with us looking down from the cross into his own ineffable Self, experiencing the disquieting inscrutability and intimate ubiquity of God's absence even more terribly than we do.

The solace we lose in the collapse of our false images of God we assuredly regain in the person of Christ, who confirms that God—while beyond all loss and pain—stands with us, knows our circumstances in the deepest way, and will continue to suffer and rejoice alongside us and all of creation in love-filled solidarity. This is the faith of Jesus Christ into which we may be ushered through experiences of God's absence. It is by this faith that the brokenness of the world is overcome (1 John 5:4), a faith I glimpsed in the words of indomitable love penned by a wounded and yet victorious woman.

I wish I could say that my answers to the intern's questions that day came easily. I wish I could report that my answers were profound, illuminating, and the perfect balance of pastoral sensibility and theological wisdom. Instead, I stood there admitting that I didn't have any answers. Yet, I believed then as now that our presence that day was important precisely because we were willing to live with the questions, pressing us to seek after God even in the deep darkness of a seven-year coma.

In one dimension, we shared in the heart-breaking, compassionate presence of God that day. In another, we were recipients of a prophetic call to faith expressed in the insistent faith of a grieving spouse. In yet another dimension, we set out on what has become for me a decade-long search into the mysterious contours of God's absence.

In the gracious disturbance of God's confounding absence we may hear God whispering, as with Elijah in the deep silence on the mountain (I Kings 19:9-13), offering divine questions in exchange for human ones: Will you still love me? Will you trust me? Will you continue to insist that I Am present in the midst of a seven-year coma—present in your insistence that I Am and in the witness of a vulnerable woman's faith pinned to a bulletin board full of cards and pictures? Will the brokenness before you and within you cause you to despair or to seek me? For if you seek me with your whole heart, you will find me (Jeremiah 29:12-14).

The Path to Peace

Repentance—a fundamental re-ordering and re-orientation of the total person—is the path to lasting peace. This is not some chimera of the punctiliar, "Damascus Road" encounter, but the submission to the call to participate in the life of God over the course of a lifetime. We forget that after Saul was knocked over, he was led blind to a process of healing and then years of retraining. Repentance is so much more than just facing some naughty behavior and disavowing it. It is so much more than a moment of decision, or assent, or cognitive realization. Repentance is a hopeful, joyful process of transformation when properly understood as much more than regret. It is the growth of the soul returning to the One to whom we belong.

Advent 2007

The Desert

read Exodus 16:1-6 & 35, 17:1-6

Desert—a place of desolation and emptiness, a wilderness.

Within the Biblical texts we see that the same word used to describe the pre-creation chaos of emptiness and void, is used again to refer to the Desert. It represented (along with the sea), in the Jewish mind, the realm of evil powers that would desire to overwhelm the ordered cosmos of Yahweh.

Being a place full of spiritual powers, the desert was no less a place where the God of gods would also be present and move in. We see this notion highlighted in biblical texts that illustrate the wandering of the people of God in the desert even as God accompanies them.

It is in the desert that God's mightiest acts of salvation and redemption were given to the people of God. It is in the desert that the tangible presence and power of God was revealed and confronted his people. It is in the desert that God shaped their identity, stripping them of the comforts of their exile so that they could be remade into the people of promise, the people of trust, the people of the blessing.

The desert is the spiritual mirror that reveals the true character of those that take the long look into that glass of desolation.

In the desert there is nothing to distract, there is no cause for excuses, and there is nothing to entice you other than you, your self and the deep desires of your heart.

The desert is an essential place of growth. Unfortunately, the idea of a "spiritual desert" gets a bad rap simply because in our values and our crass materialism we don't embrace "absence" or "lack" very well. We want productivity, not nothingness; we want stimulation, not reflection; we want sensory overload, not silence. We shrink from the silence, the absence and the reflection of the desert moments of our days, because the prospect of being alone with our thoughts—the anger, the pride, the lectures we would have given this jerk or that jerk, the petty battles, the self-indulgence, the self-pity, the self-worship, the broken self—being alone with all that, and in the presence of God no less, is just too terrifying, too honest, too real.

But we need to grow up. We need to learn that we must have hope in how we come to see and understand the Desert.

It is, undoubtedly, a place of encounter between the self and God. The experience of the desert is a non-negotiable part of us growing and becoming what God is making us.

Soren Kierkegaard—the great, Danish philosopher and Christian—writes, "Now, with God's help, I shall become myself".

The desert is where we become our true selves. The desert, the wilderness, the seeming place of disorder and chaos, is God's gracious instrument of renovation and discovery of the true self that God has dreamed for you to be.

We must see the absence and desolation of the desert through the eyes of hope. We must come to embrace the desert as undeniably essential to our faith journey and celebrate it with solemn and sober joy. Yes, celebrate the desert!

For we have an eternal perspective, the longest of long views and it is a view filled with promises and hope and joy at what we will be, with God's help.

Christ in the Desert

Read Mark 1:9-15

Christ has entered the far country of our world, being en-fleshed in the wilderness of human existence, identifying with the Creation in a full and totalizing relationship.

The mutual interiority of the Trinity is enacted between the Godhead and Creation in the person of Christ. In Christ becoming human God has identified God's self with Creation.

This is the mystery of Incarnation.

But what does this mean?

In Christ, we can no longer conceive of God as some separate entity that stands apart from ourselves and the rest of the created order, isolated and removed. The Incarnation reveals God is undeniably present to us, bound up with Creation and the illusion of divine isolation is now shattered.

It is appropriate that in Lent we consider Jesus' sojourn in the wilderness. It is in the wilderness that this Christ who comes to the far country steps even deeper into that far country in the wastes of desert.

In the Markan account of the desert sojourn (Mark 1:9-15), we are not supplied with explicit content about the testing in the desert as in Matthew and Luke's gospels.

In Mark, we hear more of the wilderness than the temptation. It is apparent that the location is more of Mark's concern as it relates to our understanding of Jesus.

The far country of the wilderness is a place of trial, danger and isolation—limited sustenance, wild animals and the like are characteristic of it. It is also the place where Satan confronts the Son of God and, as such, it is a place of spiritual peril in addition to the physical hardships he must face.

If we take the identification of God with Creation that is expressed in Christ as a filter for our reading of Mark's text, we are gifted with a wondrous picture of the hope we may have in a God who so closely identifies with the Creation that God has made.

Who among us has not felt at one time or another, or for extended seasons, or for a whole lifetime, that we ourselves reside in the exile of wilderness?

The disruption and isolation of broken marriages, the alienation of the West's electronically "connected", but relationally starved, so called technological sophistication, the lab-rat treadmill of vocational pressures, the self-hatred of late night moments before the glow of a computer or phone screen that leave us unfulfilled, and all other manner of moments and realities that threaten our wellbeing and our spiritual integrity all combine to accost our senses with the desolate facts of the darkness of our days and the even darker disposition of our hearts.

It is to that stark reality of the farthest reaches of the far country of our world that Christ is en-fleshed, God enters, and the Divine presence indwells, it takes up residence.

So as we enter the season of Lent, we must first begin with this precious truth:

Where you are, Christ has been and is.

Christ is a partaker in not just the mere victories and triumphs of life, but in every moment of our lives. God, in Christ, is not a God of just "the winners" or those who are particularly "good", "beautiful" or "right".

God is the God of the broken, the bad, the ugly and the wrong. God has come toward us. Jesus has "...suffered once for sins, the righteous for the unrighteous, to bring you to God." (IPeter 3:18a)

This is a God who does not sit on the outside in transcendent glory and bails us out of our mess. This is a God who, not knowing sin, becomes sin so that we might be healed.

Where you are, Christ has been and is.

Christ is the locus of God's self-expression and self-giving to us, a self-giving that inheres in the very nature and being of the Trinity. In Christ's identification with us in the wilderness we see God's opening of the Trinitarian life to us. In Christ's entrance to the wild wasteland he takes up into himself that wasteland, having it dwell in him, even as he dwells in it.

This is the mutually indwelling nature of God encountering our realm and that God, incredibly and simply, being God as God is. The mutuality of the Trinity is now extended to our world and to each of us.

Where you are, Christ has been and is.

It is in this God that we trust.
It is in this God who has identified with us that we identify with ourselves.

It is this very mutuality between God and Creation that we see in the covenant God establishes after the flood. This covenant is not only with humans, but with all the creation. God, as Walter Brueggemann says, "enacts a bonding of loyalty with creation" with words of "never again" and a sign of God's bow placed in the sky.

Brueggemann is rightly concerned that we do not sentimentalize or politicize "the bow" of God in the sky. The bow is symbolic of the weapons of God and hostility—that which effects isolation and division. That symbol is then symbolically hung in the sky. God has, according to Brueggemann, "made a gesture of disarmament", God has "hung up the primary weapon, and has no intention of being an aggressor or adversary". God has signaled a trade in the means and tone of relationship with the Creation and is now moving toward a "new thing" heralded in the prophets and fulfilled in Christ.

God, who is that mutually indwelling community of love that we call Trinity, indwells the creation through the incarnation of Christ, and indwells us by the Spirit. This God is not a mere partner or friend, but the Lover that envelopes and is enveloped with the Beloved to such a degree that they engulf each other, but do not consume or obliterate each other.

This is a profound, joyful reality that we must cling to lest we despair at the difficulty of the suffering and brokenness and passion of this same Christ who enacts our death with his so that we might be saved by that resurrection whose glory now shines dim and distant at this juncture of our church year.

Where you are, Christ has been and is.

After Psalm 23

"The Lord is my shepherd, I lack nothing".

There is nothing that is missing in our lives. And the pervasive sense of unrequited desire that we bear has little to do with God's capabilities or actual provision, but has everything to do with our choice of perspective.

Despite the finite boundary of our material humanity, we are beings of a transcendent nature too. We can choose to see beyond our place. We can hope. We can risk faith even as God risks faith in us.

In such risk we find ourselves participating again with God's action in the world. This faith is the life of God in action, revealed again in our choices and our deeds. It is God's life that is impossible to reserve to some abstracted ideas or notions of faith that so much of the poseur Christian exercise in America exerts its energy toward.

To live as we truly are—lacking nothing—takes immense courage because every other source of information would tell us otherwise. We are told that we lack continually and are deprived by evil people or the government or corporations or illegal immigrants or whatever the bogeyman of the hour may be. Worse some would say we are deprived by an absent, uncaring, incompetent god. And yet, it is not so.

Despite all other evidence to the contrary, we truly lack nothing when we see God rightly as our good shepherd who goes before us, leads us and cares for us. This is the mystery of our risking faith.

God reveals this faith to us. It is not delivered via experimental processes, from assembly lines or out of a wax carton you can buy at the local grocery. This is spiritual discernment of what is Real over and against the appearances of the kingdom of darkness and the human system of godless endeavor. It is the faith that is "sure of what we hope for and certain of what we do not see".

When we move to that place where we no longer can rely on our senses, our own faculties and energies, we have crossed to that place of revelation that comes by faith beyond common sense and human wisdom. It is there that we walk the "right paths" of our Shepherd and truly see that goodness and mercy surely do follow us. This mystery is rooted in the being of God—our good and loving guide. It is rooted in the heart of God whose impulse and focus is the children of His making. It is rooted in the will of God that is sovereign and sure to be seen fully one day.

Finding Our Voices

It doesn't matter anymore what the stories we've been told say about who we are. At some point we have to write our own tale. Our mothers, fathers, siblings, childhood experiences, religious leaders, home town culture, or whatever, ultimately can only say so much. And after that, if they keep speaking—as they always will—they say too much.

Resisting and telling those voices to "shut up" can only carry us so far. At some point we have to start speaking. And not just in the adolescent certainty of propositions. The "I-am-this-and-not-that" statements are only a beginning, birth pangs at best. The birth of one's self must come. At some point we have to be born to the nuance and poignant depths of story—our own story. It will be a story that will always be a work in progress, that will be interwoven with the stories of others, but will still be a tale that rises from our own voices. It will be messy, inconvenient, filled with mistakes, heresies, and stumbling, but it will be our own.

The insistence of other voices claiming to "protect" us, to know what's best for us, or to keep us from the vagaries of life are really voices of bondage—they represent an invitation to give up our birthright to ourselves and to become the means to the personal fulfillment of others by way of their domination and at the expense of our own life. Some of us cave because we are lazy.

Some of us cave because we didn't know we could say "no". Some of us cave because certain voices have co-opted God on their behalf and what higher court of appeal is there? Some of us cave because other voices are so great and powerful we think we cannot successfully resist. The reasons are many and pluriform. All must be rejected.

God has given your life to you and no one else. God has given you the freedom of your will within the human experience. Only you can exercise it on your behalf.

Life is lived toward the limit of death and limitations surround us as a reminder of this. But those voices that would add to the natural limitations of our human experience serve no valid function. They bring a kind of premature death to the divine extravagance of life. There is a boundary to the human experience but within its confines we may roam and are meant to roam. All human attempts to universally order the human experience are ultimately impositions that are soul-destroying and empty life of creative possibility. Our speaking is "self-speaking" (that is, self-defining) lest we fall into the same mode of imposition, lest we become another voice of unnatural boundary. An ethical and humane way of living takes responsibility for the self that God has enjoined you to be and become. It does not seek to speak for others and can only encourage others to do the same.

Holy Communion

Holy Communion is the Truth: it sums up the truth about God, humankind and the cosmos. It reveals God made human in the state of pure gift for us and invites us to become pure gifts for God and one another through the same celebration. All this takes place in the most humble and hidden way: the incarnate Son becomes present to us through the faith in our hearts in the form of simple bread and cup. If we accept the "logic" of God's self-emptying love, Communion becomes that luminous center which sheds new light upon all the other mysteries of faith and shows what our faith means for our communal and personal existence. When we come to this table we come to the sacred mystery of our faith, the sacred mystery of God's love.

Popular Christian writer, Rachel Held Evans says, "This is not a table for the worthy, it's a table for the hungry".

Jesus said that he didn't come for the sake of the healthy, but for those who are sick.

Here in the broken body and spilled out blood of Jesus, we see the entrance of God into our brokenness, into our disastrous wandering, and flailing and failing arrogance that streams through our relating and thinking and doing.

Here we see God doing what only God can do. For we are un-done by our sin, but God is un-doing our un-doing.

He is remaking and restoring and rescuing and redeeming us as we are spiritually nourished by the holy memory of the life, death, resurrection and return of Jesus, The Christ.

Henri Nouwen said:
"Holy Communion is recognition. It is the full realization that the one who takes, blesses, breaks, and gives is the One who, from the beginning of time, has desired to enter into communion with us. Communion is what God wants and what we want."

Every human heart, whether they realize it or not, is longing to meet this God who longs for us.

"This is not a table for the worthy, it's a table for the hungry".

I grew up in churches with a pretty flat understanding of Communion. It was loaded with a high value of control and manufactured regret.

We did communion once a month partly because "Jesus said to do it." So we did it, all the while criticizing other traditions that we believed did communion only as an empty ritual.

On the regret side, we would only talk about communion in terms of the cost of sin and how awful and bad we are. So I would find myself many times thinking that if I couldn't drum up bad feelings about myself on command, then I just didn't really respect communion or love Jesus.

Now is it important that we obey King Jesus? Yes.

Is it critical that we come to terms with the magnitude of our personal, collective, and systemic sinfulness? Absolutely.

But this is not a table that perverts the good news of Jesus by calling you to celebrate your shame as a precondition for grace. This is not a table that proclaims freedom by inviting you to inhabit bondage as your identity and destiny.

"This is not a table for the worthy, it's a table for the hungry".

We come to this table hungry for the healing and sustaining presence of a God who is reaching to us. We come to this table to be energized by His life-giving power so that we can continue and extend God's reach to all who are far from his love.

We won't miss out on the power of communion if we lose moralistic ideas of control and regret. But we will miss it if we fail to see that this table invites us to be formed, shaped and sent out as a people who together are the living presence of God's love. We will miss the power of what Christ has done and is doing if we make the body and blood of Jesus all about little 'ol me and my "get of out hell for free card" in the sweet by and by.

"This is not a table for the worthy, it's a table for the hungry".

And every time we receive God's food that relieves our hunger and longing, we are reminded of the great mass of a starving, hurting, forgotten, broken humanity who have yet to know that there is a table for the hungry, hosted by the God of the hurting, the broken hearted and the crushed in spirit. We are reminded that this town and this county is filled with people who, while they are far from God, are treasured by God who desires that they would be saved.

"This is not a table for the worthy, it's a table for the hungry".

So if you have made known your need for God, if you have accepted Jesus as the healer of your soul, if you have purposed to follow him in all your ways, if you, right now, read these words and have recognized the deep hunger of your life will be filled by Jesus, then you can come to his table and commit yourself again to Jesus who has healed you, is healing you, and will heal you for all eternity.

Praise to the Holy and Undivided Trinity, One God, Father, Son, Holy Spirit, Creator, Redeemer, Sustainer, Lover, Beloved and Love. As it was in the beginning is now and ever shall be. Alleluia. Alleluia. Amen.

Holy Saturday: The Dark Interval

Holy Saturday is the often forgotten space between the raw wound of Good Friday and the exhilarating vindication of Easter. Growing up in a low-church tradition, this day was a reprieve from the sanctified pornography that posed as a sermon about the detailed medical effects of torture and crucifixion on a human body. Back then, we'd have a communal experience of self-induced horror, and wade into some manufactured regret as we nailed pieces of paper with sins written on them to a big rough-hewn cross. On Saturday, we got to move on. We'd earned it. Since the happy ending of Resurrection was right around the corner, we all could go mow our lawn, or catch a baseball game, or whatever. Holy Saturday wasn't "holy", it was just Saturday. It was one last empty space in an already heavily edited Holy Week that gave the nod to Palm Sunday, Good Friday and Easter alone.

My love for theology, the history of Christian thought, and the classic spiritual practices of the West converged with my eventual migration from the traditions of my upbringing. These forces brought me to a place where the rich beauty of Holy Week was treasured for its power to distill the Christian message into 8 days. These days proclaim our belief in who God is and what God is all about. Moreover, this week immerses us in the power of this faith story to form us as a people who live as partners in what that God is doing for all the Creation. This new point of view meant that Holy Saturday suddenly started to matter to me. My instincts told me this day had to be more than just a warm up for Easter.

Despite the virtual absence of formal liturgy focused on the mystery of this day (our Orthodox cousins excepted), and even taking into account the late evening observance of the Great Vigil in some traditions, the silence and absence of Holy Saturday no longer represents neglect, but a profound embrace of the core apophatic character of any serious theological reflection on the persons and movement of a Triune God.

Under the shadow of Good Friday's death and dereliction, a profound crisis is presented to us today as we join with Jesus to look into the abyssal absence of God. On Holy Saturday we can rightly say that God in Christ has not only experienced the act of dying, but that God, in Christ, has plunged headlong into death. Here we confront for ourselves the paradox that the Everliving One is dead. We ourselves must wrestle with the absence of our Maker, Redeemer, Source and Friend. We now must struggle with the disruptive possibility of the loss of the One in whom we live and move and have our being. As Joan Chittister reminds us, we cannot afford to simply go about our business waiting for Exultet of The Great Vigil to pierce the darkness of Easter Eve. No. This day demands that we leave aside our love of winning, and our privileged avoidance of suffering, our immature refusal to inhabit the paradoxes of life, and our desire to impose religious certainties where they actually do not obtain for the sake of existential security that is founded on a domesticated, predictable deity of our making.

On Holy Saturday we discover the healing truth that God has inhabited death and eternally remains as much there as in the impending resurrection. In Holy Saturday we learn that, rightly understood, the experience of the absence of God is as potent an experience of God as his shining presence. The wounded longing of this Dark Interval takes us up into the wounded longing of the Son. Via negation and absence we come to know the pervasive reciprocity of the Trinity that is graciously extended to a redeemed humanity. Namely, through our own desperate and demanding cries that assert relationship, the Father, Son and Holy Spirit confirm there is no place where we can flee from their presence, there is nothing that can separate us from the Love that they are. This is the sacred and terrible conundrum of Holy Saturday.

This Dark Interval invites us to proclaim our love for the defeated, and our humble embrace of suffering, our keeping company with the ambiguity of the human experience, and our hope filled and faithful attentiveness to our ambivalence and fears for the sake of knowing the unshakeable consolations of a God who recklessly occupied death so that even there we may never be without him.

This moment points the people of God to move into the forgotten and forsaken places of failure, conflict, and dereliction around us. The absence of God gives shape to the character of the unrestrained presence of Christ in the world via The Church. That is to say, we ourselves become an open and living space that refuses any boundary or limit so that when wandering and broken humans cross the thresholds of a thousand different kinds of death they simply find Christ in his people already waiting with the healing solidarity of the God who has refused every boundary and limit, who has gone before us and inhabits all things, who fills all things through his Church, even death itself.

It is God's absence that forms us to be God's presence.

Amen.

The Feast of The Ascension

"The Ascension is a festival of the future of the world. The flesh is redeemed and glorified, for The Lord has risen for ever. We Christians are, therefore, the most sublime of materialists."

-Karl Rahner

Ascension Day is not meant to be a window into the oddities of first century cosmology. We all know we don't live in a three-tiered universe. Our affirmation of the Ascension as a matter of faith does not require some tortured obsession with reconciling the apparent difficulties that rise from divine accommodations that made the Incarnation intelligible in its original cultural context. On the other hand, I remember hearing John Shelby Spong openly deride the idea of "Spaceman Jesus" some years ago. As then, I still think these are all parts of the one massive exercise in missing the point that we call by the name "modernity".

Ascension is a profound demonstration of the deep eschatological claims and anthropological implications of the Christian witness to the resurrection. The Ascension of Jesus closes down the incipient gnosticism of otherworldly and escapist notions of Christian faith even as it deploys images of departure and supernatural power. It does this by describing the taking up the corporeal reality, the body, of the Son into the Godhead. In so doing, Ascension certifies our confidence in the salvation that comes through God's generative acts of Incarnation and Resurrection.

And while the Ascension points to these weighty theological concerns, the significance of this day is by no means an esoteric intellectual exercise rising from some fragment of equally esoteric biblical literature. For the full flowering of salvation proclaimed in the Ascension is to be embodied in the life of the Church as a continuing act of proclamation: The absence of Jesus makes room for the possibility of his presence through his people. So the liturgical and devotional function of Ascension Day is not primarily about the enthronement of Jesus as Lord, but should be regarded for its capacity to hold forth a vision of the role of the Church in the world as the "Body of Christ" which still remains on earth. This vision is distilled in the tangible signs of Eucharist as the central formative act of our worship: the Bread that is the Body of Christ sustains the Body of Christ that is the Church who bears witness to the ascended Christ as healing Lord—the one who affirms and redeems our embodied existence. Furthermore, God's embrace and reception of our materiality via the person of Christ becomes the pattern of our total acceptance and affirmation of the self-organizing complexity of the material realm in all its forms and expressions.

What this all means is the truth of Ascension is to be lived out in an earthed spirituality that joyfully embraces the deep pleasures and wonder of our lives and world, that grieves and seeks to heal and mend where disruption and despair are known, that affirms "the natural world of sea, rock and earth as being redolent with divine glory, and recognizes Christ in the faces of friends and strangers." (Christopher Irvine)

The Ascension of Jesus articulates a kind of manifesto that calls us not to rise to heavenly places of prestige, privilege and power, but to run unhindered into the embodied fullness of the human experience—to joyfully proclaim in our living that one day here on this good earth made new, in our bodies, humanity will dwell fully and freely with God precisely because God has already received us in the body of Christ.

The Trinity has purposed to make God's eternal dwelling place here with us on earth: In our eating and loving, our play and work, our laughter and our limitations. Even now the Father and Spirit commune with the risen and ascended Incarnate Son, and their communion is more sensible than we can ever conceive. That unfettered communion is our hope and carries in it the final answer to all the deepest longings of that material complex we call the human being. And lest we forget, that communion is also the reordering hope of all creation. This is the Gospel.

In the incarnated union of God and Humanity—that is, in the person of Jesus, The Christ—we discover the end and purpose of all things. That is, full communion between the Trinity and a restored humanity and creation. In the ascended Son we see the means by which the Trinity will bring their desires to fruition. The Ascension is the inauguration of this consummating delight. It marks the return and reception of the human race to our Source. And it is the harbinger of our reception of the Spirit that frees The Body that is the Church to be the vanguard of a humanity and creation repaired and made new.

Use these pages to write your own prayers.